MOUNT ST. HELENS

BY ANNETTE M. CLAYTON

Apex is distributed by North Star Editions:
sales@northstareditions.com | 888-417-0195

Produced for Apex by Red Line Editorial.

Photographs ©: Robert Krimmel/USGS, cover; Shutterstock Images, 1, 7, 15, 16–17; Harry Glicken/USGS, 4–5; Vern Hodgson/AP Images, 6, 28–29; Austin Post/USGS/AP Images, 8; USGS, 10–11; AP Images, 12–13; Jack Smith/AP Images, 14; Lyn Topinka/USGS, 18, 26–27; Donald A. Swanson/USGS, 19; AP Images, 20–21; Yakima Herald-Republic/AP Images, 22–23; Adam Mosbrucker/USGS, 24–25

Library of Congress Control Number: 2023910165

ISBN
978-1-63738-760-3 (hardcover)
978-1-63738-803-7 (paperback)
978-1-63738-886-0 (ebook pdf)
978-1-63738-846-4 (hosted ebook)

Printed in the United States of America
Mankato, MN
012024

NOTE TO PARENTS AND EDUCATORS

Apex books are designed to build literacy skills in striving readers. Exciting, high-interest content attracts and holds readers' attention. The text is carefully leveled to allow students to achieve success quickly. Additional features, such as bolded glossary words for difficult terms, help build comprehension.

TABLE OF CONTENTS

CHAPTER 1

ERUPTION!

It is May 18, 1980. An **earthquake** shakes the ground. It causes a huge landslide on Mount St. Helens. Rocks and dirt fall down the slopes.

Mount St. Helens is located in southwestern

The sideways blast of rock and ash shot out about 15 miles (24 km) from Mount St. Helens.

The side of the mountain explodes. Rocks and hot gas blast out. Mud and water flood the surrounding area.

CAVING IN

Before it **erupted**, Mount St. Helens was 9,677 feet (2,950 m) tall. Part of the mountain crumbled during the blast. It fell to 8,363 feet (2,549 m).

The eruption damaged thousands of acres of forest.

Meanwhile, ash shoots into the sky. It forms a huge cloud that blocks the sun. The day becomes dark and cold. People in nearby towns struggle to breathe.

FAST FACT

Ash poured out of the volcano for more than nine hours.

The eruption released millions of tons of ash into the air.

CHAPTER 2

HOW IT HAPPENED

Small earthquakes shook Mount St. Helens during the spring of 1980. Underground water turned to steam. This caused **pressure** to build.

Scientists expected an eruption in 1980, but they were

Rising **magma** created a bulge in the mountain. Then, on May 18, a bigger earthquake took place. It caused Mount St. Helens to erupt. Superhot rock and ash spewed out.

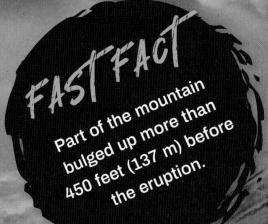

FAST FACT

Part of the mountain bulged up more than 450 feet (137 m) before the eruption.

Some of the rock and ash from Mount St. Helens was 660 degrees Fahrenheit (349°C).

More than 46 billion gallons (174 billion liters) of slush and water raced down the mountain.

Hot gas and rocks from the volcano melted snow and ice. That caused mudflows and floods. They swept over large areas of land.

LAHAR

Lahar is a mixture of water and rock pieces. It forms after a volcano erupts. The mixture pours down the sides of the volcano. It destroys everything in its path.

Lahar is very dangerous. It can flatten trees and buildings.

CHAPTER 3

MASSIVE DAMAGE

The 1980 eruption was the worst in US history. Hundreds of roads, bridges, and buildings were damaged. Fifty-seven people died.

The largest mudflow in 1980 reached about 50 miles (80 km) from Mount St. Helens.

Towns up to 300 miles (483 km) away had to shut down because of the ash.

Ash and smoke filled the air for days. It was hard for people to see and breathe. Then the ash fell and covered the ground.

TRAVELING ASH

Ash from the volcano rose 15 miles (24 km) into the air. It spread to many places and caused **pollution**. Some of the ash traveled all the way around the world.

Volcanic ash can harm peoples' eyes and lungs. It can also kill animals and plants.

FAST FACT

Some areas totally changed shape. Maps made before the eruption were no longer accurate.

The eruption harmed natural areas, too. It toppled millions of trees. Rivers filled with mud and **debris**. Some turned into lakes.

Mudflows filled riverbeds with rock and dirt. Some rivers flooded. Others were blocked.

CHAPTER 4

CLEANUP

Cleanup was a huge task. Ash from the volcano fell over 22,000 square miles (57,000 sq km). It covered the ground and blocked streets. People worked to clear it away.

Many people wore masks or bandanas to avoid
breathing in ash.

Other people worked to prevent flooding. Fallen trees filled many rivers. Crews worked to clear them. Workers also used pumps and tunnels to drain water.

After the eruption, logs covered more than 70 percent of Spirit Lake.

FAST FACT

In some places, the ash and debris were 150 feet (46 m) deep.

Scientists also studied the volcano. They observed it closely. That way, people could be more prepared if it erupted again.

Some scientists watched for new bulges in the mountain.

WARNING SIGNS

Scientists took pictures of the volcano from above. Then, they created maps. They looked for growing domes and new steam vents. Those can be signs an eruption is coming.

COMPREHENSION QUESTIONS

Write your answers on a separate piece of paper.

1. Write a few sentences explaining the main ideas of Chapter 2.

2. What part of the Mount St. Helens eruption do you find most interesting? Why?

3. How tall was the volcano before it erupted?

    A. 9,677 feet (2,950 m)

    B. 8,363 feet (2,549 m)

    C. 15 miles (24 km)

4. Why would ash filling the air make a day feel colder?

    A. The ash would bring rain.

    B. The ash would let in more sunlight.

    C. The ash would block some of the sun's heat.

5. What does **landslide** mean in this book?

*It causes a huge **landslide** on Mount St. Helens. Rocks and dirt fall down the slopes.*

    A. water spilling out from a river
    B. earth falling down from a mountain
    C. ice and snow piling up on a mountain

6. What does **accurate** mean in this book?

*Some areas totally changed shape. Maps made before the eruption were no longer **accurate**.*

    A. wrong
    B. correct
    C. able to read

Answer key on page 32.

GLOSSARY

debris
Pieces of something that broke or fell apart.

domes
Round mounds formed when lava comes to the surface.

earthquake
An event where parts of Earth shake or tremble.

erupted
Sent hot gases, ash, and lava into the air.

magma
Melted rock that is under Earth's surface.

pollution
Things that are dirty or unsafe.

pressure
A force that pushes up against something.

steam vents
Small openings where smoke or steam leaves the ground.

volcano
A mountain or hill that can shoot out lava.

BOOKS

Adamson, Thomas K. *The Eruption of Mount St. Helens.* Minneapolis: Bellwether Media, 2022.

Murray, Julie. *Volcano Eruptions.* Minneapolis: Abdo Publishing, 2023.

Schaefer, Lola. *Dangerous Volcanoes.* Minneapolis: Lerner Publications, 2022.

ONLINE RESOURCES

Visit **www.apexeditions.com** to find links and resources related to this title.

ABOUT THE AUTHOR

Annette M. Clayton is a writer living in Maryland with her husband and twin daughters. She enjoys hiking the Appalachian Trail, traveling, and writing books that teach kids about the fascinating world around them.

INDEX

ANSWER KEY:
1. Answers will vary; 2. Answers will vary; 3. A; 4. C; 5. B; 6. B